ITALIAN COOKING

CONTENTS

COLOUR LIBRARY BOOKS

INTRODUCTION

Historically, Italy is the home of good cooking. Her chefs were summoned to the French courts in the time of Louis XIII and Italian and Spanish chefs were at the court kitchens of half of Europe before the French took over with their Haute Cuisine. Today, Italian cooking is still varied and imaginative, making excellent use of simple ingredients.

Meat is expensive in Italy but fresh vegetables abound and outside the cities many Italians grow their own, so vegetable dishes are popular. Meat is "stretched" by the use of the hundreds of types of pasta available, but even these are used in different ways according to area.

All Italians love veal, and it is served in many different ways; escalopes, 'scaloppini' and 'involtini' i.e. rolled around a stuffing. Poultry is used in every region and the 'antipasta' – a plate of mixed hors d'oeuvre, with salami, olives and raw vegetables – is common to all.

Eating is always a great event in Italy, and lunch, which consists of several courses, is an important meal to which much time is devoted. Bread is served with the meal, but there is usually no butter. Wine is a must, and is often sent down the table with a carafe of water for those who want a lighter mixture. The occasion brings everybody together from the youngest children to the oldest grandparents.

It is difficult to generalise about Italian meals, because they vary so widely from region to region. In the South, where the 'durum' wheat grows best, pasta in all its forms is the basis for most meals. Maize and rice grow well in the rich plains of the North, so risotto and polenta are common staples.

In the North people often cook with butter, while in the South, olive oil is more frequently used. The people of the south, who keep their cattle for farm work and dairy products, eat less meat than their wealthier cousins in the north. There are many variations within this broad outline, but the one thing all the regions of Italy have in common is a joyful approach to food and cooking. Italian gastronomy stands at the crossroads of East and West and all Mediterranean countries have a common link with Italian cookery where the accent is on vivid colours and warm appetising food.

Anchovy Puffs

Bread and Tomato Soup

Anchovy Puffs

Donzelline Ripiene di Accuighe

½ stick butter	¼ cup, anchovy fillets,
1 cup all-purpose flour	chopped
milk	olive oil

Cut butter into flour until particles are very fine. Stir in enough milk to make a stiff dough. Knead on a floured surface until a smooth ball. Cover and chill for 30 minutes. Divide into two equal parts. Roll both out thinly. Scatter the anchovies over one piece of dough. Cover with the other half and roll out again, as thinly as possible. Cut into small triangles, discarding any pieces without anchovy. Heat a little olive oil in a large frying pan and fry the 'puffs' quickly till golden on both sides. Add more oil when necessary. Serve hot.

Bread and Tomato Soup

Pappa al Pomodoro

½ lb firm type white bread,	2 cloves garlic, chopped
crusts removed	2 tbsp basil, chopped
1 lb tomatoes	salt and pepper
5 cups chicken broth	olive oil for serving

Roughly chop the bread and soak in water to cover f 30 minutes. Drain and squeeze very thoroughly. Pe the tomatoes, remove seeds and finely chop. Bring tl broth to a boil in a large saucepan. Stir in the brea chopped tomatoes, garlic and basil. Season with s and pepper. Cook, covered, for 10-15 minutes. Har oil round separately when serving.

Hot Vegetable Dip

Bagna cauda

3 cloves garlic	¼ cup anchovies in oil,
1 cup olive oil	chopped

Cut garlic cloves into very thin strips and saute them in oil until soft. Keep garlic from browning and consequently losing its flavour. Remove pan from heat and add anchovies. Crush anchovies with wooden spoon. Replace on heat and keep hot.

This "bagna cauda," as it is known in Piedmontese dialect, is served in the pan in which it is made, which should ideally be a glazed earthenware bowl, called a

"fojot," which is kept hot either with coals or over a ve low chafing-dish flame. The bagna cauda is placed the centre of the table and each person dips strips of ra or very slightly cooked vegetables into it. The class vegetable used by the Piedmontese is the cardoon, b you may use any of the following: green peppers, ra slightly parboiled or in oil; or, (again, raw or slight cooked) celery, cabbage, Jerusalem artichok potatoes, etc.

A refinement of bagna cauda calls for adding, ju before using, a few tablespoons of heavy cream and thinly sliced white truffle.

Hot Vegetable Dip

SOUPS/ANTIPASTI

Tuna Stuffed Eggs

Stracciatella Soup

Tuna Stuffed Eggs

Uova Sode con Tonno

5 eggs
4 oz can drained tuna
3 tbsp mayonnaise
1 tbsp light cream

parsley or chopped olives to garnish
salt and pepper

Hard cook the eggs. Shell and cut each egg lengthwise in half. Using a spoon remove yolks without breaking whites. Put yolks through a sieve into a mixing bowl. Add the tuna, mayonnaise, and cream. Mix ingredients well until smooth. Season with salt and pepper. Stuff the egg whites neatly with the mixture. Decorate each with the chopped parsley or olives.

Stracciatella Soup

2 eggs
2 tbsp grated Parmesan cheese
2 tbsp fresh white breadcrumbs
2 tbsp clarified butter

nutmeg
salt and pepper
5 cups chicken broth
2 tbsp chopped parsley

Mix together the eggs, cheese, breadcrumbs, clarified butter and nutmeg. Season with salt and pepper and stir in ½ cup chicken broth. Bring the remaining broth to the boil, pour on the egg mixture, all at once. Whisk vigorously with a fork. Add the parsley. Bring to a boil again and serve at once.

Milanese thick soup

Minestrone alla milanese

4 strips bacon
¼ lb bacon rind (½ cup chopped)
1 bunch parsley, chopped
1 clove garlic, chopped
1 stalk celery, chopped
2 potatoes, chopped
2 carrots, chopped
1 zucchini, chopped

1 cup (¼ lb) ½-inch pieces, green beans
1 cup dried borlotti beans or navy beans
3 tomatoes, peeled and diced
salt
1 cup coarsely grated savoy cabbage
1 cup (½ lb) natural rice

Chop bacon extremely fine until it is almost a pulp. Place bacon, bacon rind, parsley, garlic, and celery in a soup pot. Saute 5 minutes. Add potatoes, carrots, zucchini, green beans, beans and tomatoes. Cover with water and season to taste with salt. Bring to a boil over high heat, lower heat and simmer covered for at least 2 hours. Add water from time to time to keep up level of liquid. After first hour add cabbage. Thirty minutes before serving add natural rice and simmer, being careful to keep rice al dente. Remove bacon rind and season to taste with salt. Serve with or without a little grated Parmesan cheese.

Toasted Mozzarella Sandwiches

Omelette Soup

Toasted Mozzarella Sandwiches

Mozzarella in carrozza all'italiana

2 balls, mozzarella cheese	2 eggs
8 slices firm type white bread, crusts trimmed	salt
milk, about 1-1½ cups	2 tbsp butter
flour	⅓ cup olive oil

Slice mozzarella into ½-inch thick slices. Dip slices of bread into milk removing them quickly so that they are barely softened. Place a slice of mozzarella between each pair of bread slices and press gently between your hands. Cut each sandwich into 2 rectangles. Flour sandwiches lightly and then dip into eggs beaten with a pinch of salt. Fry sandwiches in butter and oil in a large frying pan; wait until oil and butter are very hot before you put sandwiches in. Fry until brown, turn and brown on other side. Remove and drain on paper towels. Serve on a preheated platter covered with a napkin. This "mozzarella in carrozza" can be made more zestful by including pieces of anchovy fillets between mozzarella and bread.

Omelette Soup

Minestra di Frittata

4 eggs	salt and pepper
1 cup fresh white breadcrumbs	2 tbsp butter
3 tbsp chopped parsley	6 cups chicken broth
1 tsp chopped marjoram	grated Parmesan cheese to serve

Beat the eggs well and stir into them the breadcrumbs, 2 tbsp parsley and marjoram. Sprinkle with salt and pepper. Heat the butter in a medium frying pan. Pour in enough egg mixture to make a very thin omelette. As soon as it is golden on one side, turn and cook on the other. Transfer to a plate. Continue until all egg mixture has been used. In a large pan bring the chicken broth to the boil. Season with salt and pepper. While it is heating, roll each omelette up tightly. Cut into very thin slices. When broth is boiling add the omelette slices. Heat for 1-2 minutes. Serve with remaining parsley and Parmesan cheese.

Gourmet Mushrooms

Funghi del 'Gourmet'

¾ lb cultivated mushrooms	16 asparagus tips, cooked and drained
3 artichoke hearts, sliced thin	¾ cup mayonnaise
juice of 1 lemon	2 tbsp olive oil
1 white celery heart, cut into strips	2 ripe tomatoes, peeled and pressed through a sieve
½ lb shrimps, cooked, shelled and de-veined	salt

Peel mushroom caps, simmer for 15 minutes in water to cover. Drain them well. Sprinkle artichoke hearts with half the lemon juice to keep them from darkening. Put mushrooms, topped with artichokes, celery, shrimp and asparagus in little piles in a large glass bowl. Chill. Mix mayonnaise with oil, remaining lemon juice and tomato pulp. Add salt to taste. Serve this sauce with vegetables.

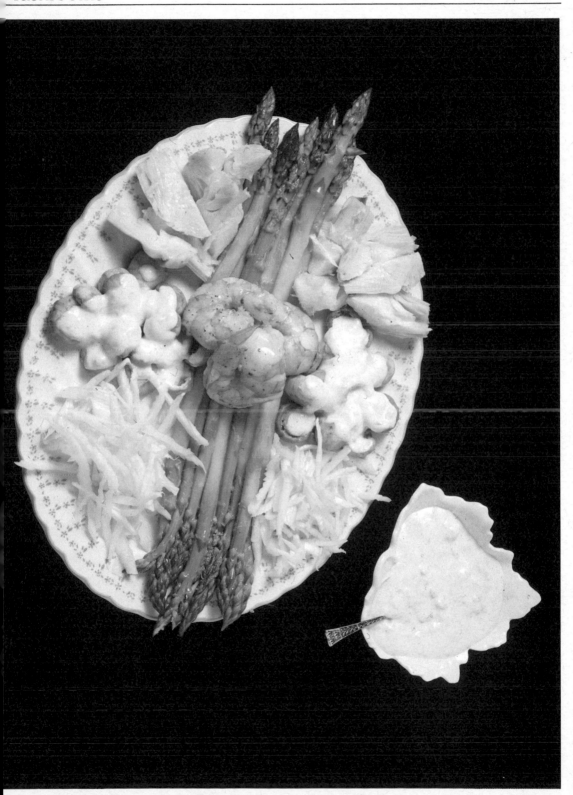

Ravioli with Spinach & Cheese

Straw and Hay

Ravioli with Spinach & Cheese

Ravioli con spinaci e formaggio

Filling: –
1 cup cooked spinach
1 tbsp butter
1 cup ricotta cheese
½ egg
salt, pepper and nutmeg

Basic pasta receipe: –
¾ cup all-purpose flour
salt
1 egg
2 tbsp water
to serve:-
½ stick butter
6 tbsp light cream
grated Parmesan cheese

Chop the spinach finely. In a small pan heat the butter and saute the spinach for 2-3 minutes. Press the ricotta through a sieve into a mixing bowl. Mix in the egg and spinach. Season with salt, pepper and nutmeg.

For the pasta, put the flour and salt on a floured board, make a hollow in the centre, and break in the egg. Mix with a fork until the egg has been absorbed. Gradually add enough cold water to make a soft clay-like ball of dough. Knead on a floured surface, until elastic. About 10 minutes. Cover and rest for 1 hour. Roll out half the dough at a time. Place tsps of filling in mounds, 1-1½ inches apart on the dough. Roll out second half of dough, and brush with extra beaten egg. Place dough, egg side down over filling. Cut into 1½-inch squares with a fluted pastry cutter. Press edges well together. Dry for several hours on a clean dry, towel.

Cook in boiling salted water for about 10 minutes. While they are cooking heat 2-3 oz butter in a medium pan, stir in 2-3 tbsp light cream. Remove from heat. Drain ravioli, put into warmed serving dish. Pour over butter mixture. Sprinkle with Parmesan cheese. Broil for 5-10 minutes until well browned. Serve with more Parmesan cheese.

Straw and Hay

Paglia e fieno

½ lb white taglierini
½ lb green taglierini
butter

salt
grated Parmesan to serve
fresh tomato sauce (optiona

Boil the taglierini in two separate pans of boiling salte water. It will be ready very quickly. Drain and mix th two together, adding enough butter to prevent the past from sticking. Serve with plenty of butter and grate Parmesan, tomato sauce too if desired.

Neopolitan Pizza

Pizza Napoletana

Pizza dough made with 4½
  cups all-purpose flour
2 cups chopped tomato pulp
  (skin and seeds removed)
  or 1 can peeled Italian
  tomatoes, drained, seeds
  removed and chopped

1 lb mozzarella cheese
1 can (2 oz) anchovies or 4
  salted anchovies
1 tsp crumbled oregano
¼ cup olive oil

On a greased baking sheet stretch out dough larg enough to make a 14-inch round. Pinch edge to make rim. Cover with chopped tomato and slices of moz zarella. Arrange anchovies like a lattice on top of cheese Sprinkle on oregano and oil. Bake in a preheated ove 400°F for 30-40 minutes. Serve piping hot from th oven.

Neopolitan Pizza

PASTA/PIZZA/RICE

Spaghetti with Pesto Genovese

Tagliatelle with Dried Mushrooms and Cream

Spaghetti with Pesto Genovese

Spaghetti con pesto genovese

3 medium potatoes	¼ cup pine nuts
1 lb spaghetti	salt
olive oil	¼ cup grated Parmesan
For the Pesto: –	cheese
¼ cup basil leaves	1¼ cups olive oil
2 cloves garlic, chopped	

Peel the potatoes, and cut them into small dice. Put them in a large pan of boiling salted water with 2 tbsp oil and boil for 5 minutes. Add the spaghetti and continue to boil until both are cooked. (The potato should remain quite firm).

While they are cooking, make the Pesto. Mash the basil together in a mortar with the garlic, pine nuts, and a pinch of salt. Add the Parmesan cheese a little at a time. Finally beat in the oil very slowly until well blended.

Drain the potatoes and spaghetti. Stir in 2 tbsp olive oil, and 2 tbsp pesto. Put into a warmed serving dish and hand round the remaining pesto and more Parmesan cheese.

Tagliatelle with Dried Mushrooms and Cream

Tagliatelle con funghi secchi e panna

¼ cup dried mushrooms or	½ cup light cream
½ lb fresh	4 tbsp grated Parmesan
3 tbsp olive oil	cheese
1 medium onion, chopped	2 tbsp chopped parsley
1 lb tagliatelle	salt and pepper

Soak the dried mushrooms in water for 2-3 hours. Drain and squeeze out the liquid. Roughly chop. Heat the oil in a small pan and saute the chopped onion for 1-2 minutes. Add the mushrooms and saute for a further 10 minutes. Meanwhile cook the tagliatelle in boiling salted water. Drain and return to the pan. Stir in the mushrooms, cream, cheese and parsley. Season well with salt and pepper. Stir until heated and well combined. Serve at once.

Risotto Milanese

Risotto alla milanese

½ cup butter	1 tsp crumbled saffron
2 tbsp chopped beef marrow	4 cups (1 quart) chicken
½ small onion, chopped	broth, (approx.)
salt, pepper	½ cup grated Parmesan
½ cup dry white wine	
2 cups (1 lb) rice	

Melt half of the butter in a saucepan. Add beef marrow, onion and a pinch each of salt and pepper. When onion is tender but not brown, add wine and let it boil until half its original volume. Stir in rice. Dissolve saffron in broth and add to pan. Stir to keep rice from sticking. When broth is simmering stir occasionally and cook until rice is cooked al dente and liquid is absorbed. Add more broth from time to time, if necessary, to prevent sticking. Stir in remaining butter and grated Parmesan. Let stand over very low heat for a few minutes, then serve with Ossi Buchi.

Risotto
Milanese

PASTA/PIZZA/RICE

Stuffed Pancakes

Tortellini with Butter and Cheese

Stuffed Pancakes

Crespolini

1 tbsp butter	10-12 pancakes, about 5″ in
2-3 chicken livers	diameter
4 oz cooked spinach	sauce
4 oz ricotta cheese	½ stick butter
1 oz grated Parmesan cheese	2 oz all-purpose flour
1 egg	2 cups milk
salt and pepper	salt and pepper

Melt the butter in a small pan and saute the livers for 3-4 minutes. Chop them finely, mix with the chopped spinach, ricotta cheese and Parmesan. Add the beaten egg and season with salt and pepper.

Put 2-3 tbsp filling in each pancake and roll up tightly. Place side by side in a shallow baking pan. Make the sauce with the butter, flour and milk, season well. Pour over the pancakes and finish with a sprinkle of more Parmesan cheese. Cook at 400°F for 15-20 minutes.

Tortellini with Butter and Cheese

Tortellini con Burro e Formaggio

6 cups chicken broth	grated Parmesan cheese to
1½ lb tortellini	serve
1 stick butter	

Bring the broth to a boil, gently drop in the tortellini and simmer for 20 minutes. While the pasta is cooking, heat the butter in a medium pan. Continue to heat the butter until it begins to turn a light brown. Remove at once from the heat. Drain the tortellini put them in a warmed vegetable dish and pour the butter over. Serve with the grated Parmesan cheese.

Sherrie's Pizza

Pizza dough made with 4½ cups all-purpose flour	½ lb pepperoni sausage, sliced
1½ cups chopped tomato pulp	1 small green capsicum
½ lb chopped, sliced mushrooms	1 cup grated mozzarella cheese
black and green olives	¼ cup grated Parmesan cheese

On a greased baking sheet stretch out dough large enough to make a 14″ round. Pinch edge to make a rim. Cover with chopped tomato pulp, mushrooms, olives, sausage and chopped capsicum. Sprinkle over Mozzarella and Parmesan. Bake in a pre-heated oven 400°F for 30-40 minutes. Serve piping hot from the oven.

Sherrie's
Pizza

PASTA/PIZZA/RICE

Rice Salad
Roman style

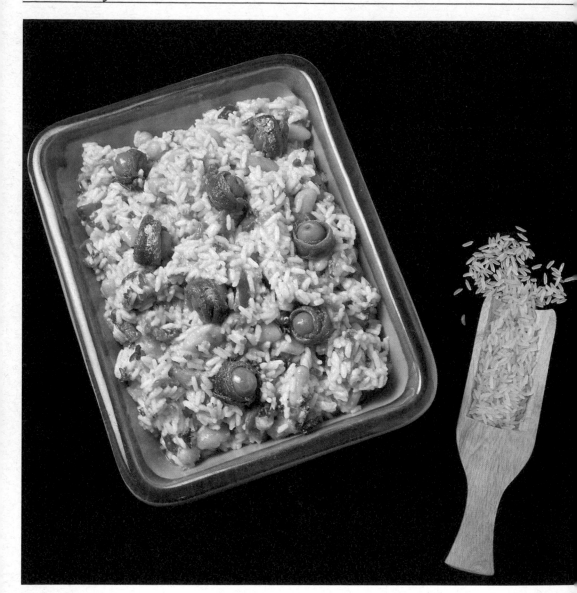

Rice Salad Roman style

Insalata di riso alla romana

1 cup (½ lb) rice
⅔ cup uncooked cannellini
  beans
2 cloves garlic
½ tsp red pepper flakes
½ cup soft breadcrumbs
  soaked in ¼ cup beef
  broth and squeezed dry
½ cup oil
3 tbsp red wine vinegar
1 tsp salt
⅓ cup diced lean prosciutto
  crudo

4 slices slab bacon
1 can flat anchovy fillets,
  rinsed with cold water
8 large green olives
2 tbsp coarsely chopped
  fresh basil leaves
2 tbsp coarsely chopped
  fresh marjoram

Cook rice and beans separately in lightly salted wate
until tender. Drain and cool. Grind garlic and ho
pepper in a mortar, add squeezed breadcrumbs an
beat in oil, wine vinegar and salt. Put rice and beans in
salad bowl. Add prosciutto. Cut bacon into thin strip
and saute in 1 tablespoon oil until crisp. Drain bacon an
add to salad bowl. Stir in bread sauce. Roll anchov
fillets around olives and arrange them on top of salad a
decoration. Sprinkle with basil and marjoram cut int
rather large pieces. Chill. Serve either as a luncheo
dish or as antipasto.

Lasagne with Four Cheeses

PASTA/PIZZA/RICE

Lasagne with Four Cheeses

Lasagne con quatro formaggi

tbsp olive oil
lb green lasagne
stick butter
tbsp all-purpose flour
/4 cups milk

6 tbsp grated Parmesan
  cheese
¼ cup grated gruyere cheese
¼ cup mozzarella, diced
¼ cup pecorino, diced
salt, pepper and nutmeg

ll a large pan with salted water. Add the olive oil. Cook
e lasagne 4 or 5 leaves at a time for 7-10 minutes. Lift
ach batch out carefully, plunge into cold water. When
l the pasta has been cooked, drain well on absorbent
per.

Make a bechamel sauce with the butter, flour and milk. Add the cheeses to the sauce, reserving 2 tbsp Parmesan. Season with salt, pepper and nutmeg. Stir until cheeses have melted.

Butter generously a deep baking pan. Put in alternate layers of lasagne and sauce: there should be at least four layers. Finish with a layer of sauce, sprinkle with the reserved grated Parmesan. Cook at 350°F for 45 minutes until bubbling and golden brown.

Fresh Sardines Ligurian Style

Sole with Pine Nuts

Fresh Sardines Ligurian Style

Sarde fritte alla ligure

16 fresh sardines	1 clove garlic, chopped
¼ cup dried mushrooms, soaked and chopped	several sprigs chopped fresh marjoram
olive oil	pinch oregano
salt and pepper	3 eggs
4 slices stale white bread	all-purpose flour
milk	dry breadcrumbs
1 tbsp grated Parmesan cheese	

Clean sardines, discarding heads and tails. Slit open on one side but without separating halves. Carefully remove bones. Saute mushrooms in 2 tbsp oil. Sprinkle with a little salt and place in a bowl. Soak the stale bread in milk. Wring it out well, then add it to the mushrooms with Parmesan, garlic, marjoram, oregano, 1 egg and a pinch of salt. Mix well. Put a little of the mixture into each sardine. Coat each sardine with flour. Dip into the remaining beaten eggs and then into the breadcrumbs, pressing firmly. Fry in hot oil ¼" deep until brown on both sides. Serve piping hot.

Sole with Pine Nuts

Soqliole alla Veneziana

8 fillets of sole, skinned	½ cup water
all-purpose flour	½ lb white grapes, halved
2 tbsp olive oil	and pipped
½ stick butter	2 tbsp pine nuts
½ cup white wine vinegar	salt and pepper

Coat the fish lightly in flour. Heat the oil and butter in large frying pan. Saute the fish gently until golden brown on both sides. Add more oil or butter if necessary. Place the fillets on a serving dish and keep warm. Add to the frying pan the white wine vinegar, water, grapes and pine kernels; season, and simmer gently for 5 minutes, until the liquid has almost evaporated. Pour the contents of the pan over the fish and serve.

Herb Stuffed Mackerel

Sgombro Ripieno

1 medium mackerel	1 tsp chopped onion
1 small sprig rosemary	2 tbsp white wine
1 tsp chopped thyme	1 tbsp olive oil
3 tbsp chopped parsley	salt and pepper

Clean the fish but leave the head and tail on. Stuff the body of the mackerel with the rosemary, thyme, parsley and onion. Lay the fish in a shallow baking pan, pour over the white wine, and olive oil. Sprinkle with salt and pepper. Bake, uncovered, at 350°F for 20-25 minutes. Garnish with more fresh sprigs of rosemary and thyme.

Herb Stuffed Mackerel

FISH

Fish with Marsala

Oysters au Gratin

Fish with Marsala

Pesce al Marsala

1 lb fillets sole	4 tbsp Marsala
1 small onion	1 lemon
seasoned flour	salt and pepper
2 tbsp oil for frying	

Skin the sole. Boil the skin for 15 minutes in a little water, with the sliced onion to make 4-5 tbsp broth. Lightly flour the fish fillets. Heat the oil in a large frying pan. Saute the fish on both sides until golden. Add the Marsala and the strained fish broth. Cook gently for a further 10 minutes. Cut the lemon in two, squeeze the juice of one half onto the fish. season with salt and pepper. Place the fish fillets on a warmed serving platter. Pour over the pan juices. Garnish with the remaining half lemon cut into slices.

Oysters au Gratin

Ostriche au gratinate

3 cloves garlic, chopped	24 fresh oysters
⅔ cup dry white	6 tbsp butter
breadcrumbs	¼ cup grated Parmesan
black peppercorns	cheese

Mix garlic with half of the breadcrumbs and a goo pinch of freshly ground black pepper. Open oyster she and remove oysters. Brush a shallow 1½ quart cass role with half of the butter. Cover bottom with brea crumbs and garlic mixture. Top with oysters. Sprink with grated Parmesan and remaining breadcrumbs. D with remaining butter. Bake in a pre-heated oven 400 for 10-15 minutes or until brown. Serve immediately.

Salmon Trout with Garlic Sauce

Trota salmonata con agliata

Court bouillon:	2 lb salmon trout, cleaned
1 cup water	with head and tail left on
1 cup dry white wine	1 lb potatoes, diced
1 carrot, chopped	4 cloves garlic, chopped
1 rib celery, chopped	1 cup soft breadcrumbs
1 sprig parsley, chopped	2 tbsp wine vinegar
1 small onion, chopped	salt and pepper
salt	7 tbsp olive oil
4 peppercorns	2 lemons
juice of ½ lemon	¼ cup melted butter

Combine all the ingredients for the court bouillon, bri to a boil and simmer for 5 minutes. Place trout in a fi kettle, cover with court bouillon. Bring to a boil, simm for 12 minutes. Boil potatoes in salted water un tender. Grind garlic in a mortar, add bread soaked vinegar, salt and pepper. Add oil, drop by drop and be until smooth. Drain trout, transfer to a platter. Garni with lemon halves and surround with boiled potato mixed with melted butter. Spoon over garlic sauce.

Salmon Trout
with Garlic Sauce

FISH

Squid Bari Style

Mussels on the Half Shell

Squid Bari Style

Calamaretti alla barese

2 lbs small squid	2 cups sieved tomato pulp
2 cloves garlic chopped	salt and pepper
⅔ cup olive oil	6 sprigs parsley, chopped

Clean squid. Wash repeatedly in cold running water and separate sac and tentacles. Saute garlic in 7 tbsp of the oil, add tomato pulp. Season with salt and pepper and simmer sauce for about 10 minutes. In another pan, saute squid in remaining oil, turning constantly. Pour the sauce over the squid and simmer covered, for 1 hour or until the squid are tender. Sprinkle chopped parsley over dish and serve.

Mussels on the Half Shell

Cozze crude al limone

3½ lbs mussels	peppercorns
2 lemons	

Clean mussels with a stiff brush, wash thoroughly unde cold running water. Open with a clam knife and serv them on the half shell with lemon quarters. Pas peppermill so each person may season to taste wit freshly ground black pepper.

Deviled Lobster Italian Style

Aragoste alla diavola all'italiana

2 live lobsters, about 1½ lb each	salt and pepper
3 tbsp butter	2 tbsp olive oil
1 tbsp brown mustard	3 tbsp dry breadcrumbs
¼ cup brandy	2 lemons sliced

Drop lobsters into boiling salted water. When water re-boils boil for 5 minutes. Drain and drench with cold water. Cut lobsters in half lengthwise, crack legs and claws. Remove "sand sack" and dark coloured intestine. Reserve coral and tomalley. Mix butter until it is creamy. Stir in mustard and creamy parts of lobster after pressing them through a sieve. Light brandy in a cup and pour flaming over mixture. When flames die, sprinkle with salt and pepper and mix thoroughly. Brush a baking dish with oil. Add lobster halves cut side up. Spread some of the mustard sauce over them. Bake in preheated oven 375°F for about 15 minutes, basting from time to time with pan juices. Meanwhile mix breadcrumbs with remaining mustard sauce. Remov pan from oven and spread this mixture over lobste halves. Bake for a further 5 minutes until well-browned Place on serving platter with shredded lettuce and lemon slices. Pour over pan juices and serve.

Deviled Lobster
Italian Style

FISH

Fish Stew

Fried Squid

Fish Stew

Cacciucco alla livornese

1 medium mackerel, cleaned	1 bayleaf
½ lb halibut	½ cucumber
2 fillets lemon sole	½ lb tomatoes, skinned and
½ lb scampi, cooked, shelled	seeded
and de-veined	4 tbsp white wine
4 tbsp olive oil	1¼ cups water
1 medium onion	4 slices French bread
2 cloves garlic, chopped	salt, pepper and sugar
2 tbsp chopped parsley	

Skin and fillet the mackerel, discarding head and tail. Cut into thin, bite sized slices. Cut the halibut into bite-sized pieces, the sole into 1″ strips. Heat the oil in a large frying pan, saute the sliced onion and garlic, for 2-3 minutes. Add the parsley, bayleaf, diced cucumber, and chopped tomatoes. Saute for 1-2 minutes then add the wine, water and seasoning. Cover and simmer gently for 20 minutes. Add all the fish except the scampi, with a little more water if necessary. Cover and simmer for a further 10 minutes. Add the scampi for the last 5 minutes. Meanwhile, bake the bread slowly in a medium oven, rub with a piece of cut garlic. Put one slice in the base of each serving plate, pour the stew over. Garnish with more chopped parsley before serving.

Fried Squid

Calamaretti fritti

2 lbs small squid	salt
all-purpose flour	2 lemons cut in halves
deep oil, heated to 360°F	

Clean squid. Remove skin. Wash in cold running water and separate sac and tentacles. Cut into bite-sized pieces. Coat with flour lightly and deep fry in oil until golden brown. Season with salt, arrange on a serving platter and garnish with lemon halves.

Barbecued Whiting Sardinian Style

Naselli alla brace alla sardegnola

2 whitings weighing about	salt, pepper
2½ lbs	olive oil
bay leaves	

Clean whiting, discard head, cut each fish into 4 crosswise pieces. Spear pieces on heatproof shewers, alternating whiting with bay leaves. Season with salt, pepper and brush with oil. Cook 6 inches above gray charcoal, basting as needed with oil until fish is cooked, about 10 to 15 minutes.

Barbecued Whiting
Sardinian Style

Braised Oxtail Cowherd Style

Lamb Chops Calabrian

Braised Oxtail Cowherd Style

Coda alla vaccinara

1 oxtail, weighing about
    4½ lb
2 bay leaves
2 carrots, chopped
4 cups sliced celery
½ lb lean bacon chopped
¼ cup chopped prosciutto
    crudo
1 onion chopped

1 cup dry white wine
2 cups chopped tomato pulp,
    skin and seeds removed
    and sieved
beef broth
pinch powdered cinnamon
salt and pepper

Cut the tail into pieces and soak in cold water for at least 2 hours. Bring water to a boil with a bouquet garni consisting of bay leaves, 1 of the carrots and ½ cup of the celery. Boil oxtail for 1 hour, skimming occasionally. Drain. Saute bacon, prosciutto crudo, remaining carrot and onion until golden. Add oxtail and brown for 10 minutes, then pour in wine and simmer until it evaporates. Add tomato pulp to pan. Cover and continue cooking for about 3 hours over low heat, adding a little broth as needed. Dice remaining celery and cook for 10 minutes in boiling salted water. Drain and add to oxtail about ½ hour before completion of cooking. Season with a pinch of cinnamon, salt and a little freshly ground pepper just before serving.

Lamb Chops Calabrian

Costolettine di agnello alla Calabrese

8 loin or rib lamb chops
salt and pepper
all-purpose flour
5 tbsp oil
8 anchovy fillets

2 tbsp capers
½ cup canned mushrooms,
    drained
½ cup canned artichoke
    hearts in oil, drained

Pound chops to flatten slightly. Sprinkle with salt an pepper. Dip into flour. Heat oil and brown chops for 2- minutes on each side over high heat. Drain on pape towelling. Arrange on a serving platter and garnish wit anchovy fillets, capers, mushrooms and artichok hearts.

Saddle of Pork Tuscan Style

Arista di maiale

2½ lbs pork joint
2 cloves garlic, cut into slivers
2 sprigs fresh rosemary

salt, peppercorns
4 tbsp olive oil

Cut small slits in pork and stuff with slivers of garlic an tufts of rosemary. Season with salt and freshly groun pepper. Heat 2 tbsp of the oil in a roasting pan. Ad pork, pour a thin stream of remaining oil over it an roast in preheated oven 425°F for about 20 minute When pork is nicely browned, lower heat to 350°F an roast for another 1¼ hours, turning meat occasionall Remove from oven, carve, arrange slices on a servin platter and serve. This dish is good either hot or cold.

Saddle of Pork
Tuscan Style

MEATS

- 28 -

Saltimbocca: Veal, Prosciutto & Sage

Beef Scallops Tuscan Style

Saltimbocca: Veal, Prosciutto & Sage

Saltimbocca alla romana

8 slices veal scallopini
8 slices prosciutto crudo
8 fresh sage leaves
1 tbsp butter

¼ cup olive oil
salt
1 cup dry white wine

On each slice of veal place a slice of prosciutto crudo and a sage leaf and fasten with a toothpick. Melt butter and oil in a frying pan. Brown veal on both sides. Sprinkle with salt and add wine. Simmer for about 10 minutes. Remove veal and place on a platter. Boil pan juices until reduced to half their original volume. Pour pan juices over veal.

Beef Scallops Tuscan Style

Scaloppine alla toscana

1½ lb boneless beef round,
   sliced ¼" thick
salt
all-purpose flour
1 egg, beaten
1½ tbsp butter

2 tbsp olive oil
⅓ cup Marsala
1 tbsp tomato paste
4 anchovy fillets, chopped
1 tbsp capers, chopped

Pound beef very thin, sprinkle with salt and flour on both sides. Dip in beaten egg. Heat butter and oil in a large frying pan. Brown beef slices on both sides. Add Marsala, raise heat slightly, and simmer until wine evaporates. Place beef slices on a platter and keep warm. Into same pan, add tomato paste mixed with ½ cup water and simmer for 5 minutes. Add anchovies and capers and simmer 2 minutes more. Put beef back in pan with sauce and simmer 2-3 minutes over a low heat. Garnish with rolled up anchovies with capers in the centre.

Calf's Liver Venetian Style

Fegato di vitello alla veneziana

Venice claims to have invented the combination of liver and onions; there is no place which cooks it better!

½ lb onions, sliced
⅓ cup olive oil
1¼ lb calf's liver

salt and pepper
2 lemons, cut into wedges

Fry the onions in the oil until golden brown, stirring constantly. Cut liver into thin slices, removing membranes and other tough portions. Season with freshly ground pepper and add to pan. Cook for a few minutes until brown on both sides. Sprinkle with salt and turn out onto a hot platter. Garnish with lemon wedges.

Calf's Liver
Venetian Style

MEATS

Roman
Meatballs

Sicilian
Roast Lamb

Roman Meatballs
Polpette romane

1 lb mozzarella (or scamorza),
  grated
1 cup milk
½ cup (¼ lb) minced baked,
  or boiled ham
salt

2¼ cups all purpose flour
2 eggs
⅔ cup grated Parmesan
  cheese
½ cup butter

In a saucepan mix flour, eggs and Parmesan. Gradually
stir in milk. Set saucepan over a low heat and beat in half
of the butter and a pinch of salt. Cool. Turn dough onto
a floured board and knead a few times until it becomes a
smooth ball.

Take 2 tbsp of ham and mozarella and, using the
palms of your hands, roll it into a ball about as large as a
walnut. Pinch off pieces of dough and flatten to ¼″
thickness. Wrap ball in dough to cover it completely.
Continue until you have used up all the ham and all the
dough. Butter a shallow baking pan, put in meatballs in
a single layer. Dot each with a bit of remaining butter.
Bake in a pre-heated oven for about 30 minutes or until
brown.

Sicilian Roast Lamb
Agnello al forno

1 leg of lamb, about 3½ lb in
  weight
¼ cup boiled ham, diced
1-2 sprigs rosemary

1 stick butter
3 tbsp soft breadcrumbs
½ lb grated cheese
salt and pepper

With a sharp knife, make incisions into the surface of the
lamb, about 1″ deep. Into each cut push a piece of ham
and two or three leaves of rosemary. Put the meat into a
large baking pan, season with salt and pepper and pour
over the melted butter. Mix the breadcrumbs and the
grated cheese and spread evenly over the meat
pressing down well. Roast in a pre-heated oven 375°F
basting from time to time, for about 1½ hours. (If you
have any cooked meat left over, it is delicious used in
lasagne).

Skewered Veal Birds
Oseleti scampai

½ lb lean veal steak, cubed
½ lb fresh ham steak cubed
¼ lb pork liver, cubed
¼ lb bacon, cubed

fresh sage leaves
3 tbsp oil
7 tbsp dry white wine
½ cup chicken broth

Put veal, ham, liver and bacon cubes on long skewers,
alternating various kinds of meat and occasionally
putting a sage leaf between one piece and another. Heat
oil in a frying pan, add skewers and cook over high heat,
turning occasionally. Add white wine and broth and
cook for another 10 minutes, turning occasionally.
Serve on a bed of polenta.

Skewered
Veal Birds

MEATS

Veal with Tuna

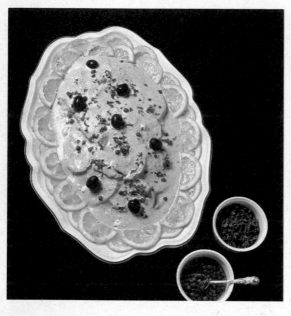

Filet Mignon Piquant

Veal with Tuna

Vitello tonnato

1¼ lbs boneless breast or shoulder of veal, in one piece	½ cup flaked tuna
	1 cup mayonnaise
salt	2 tbsp capers
1 rib celery, chopped	2 anchovy fillets in oil
1 carrot	½ cup dry white wine
2 tbsp chopped parsley	1 lemon, cut into slices
1 tbsp chopped onion	1 carrot, sliced and cooked
	2 pickled gherkins

Trim membranes from veal. Put a little water and a few pinches of salt in a saucepan; add celery, carrot, parsley and onion. Heat, and when the water comes to a boil add veal. Simmer 1 to 1½ hours or until veal is tender. Drain and set aside to cool. Put tuna through a food mill and blend it with mayonnaise, half of the capers and anchovy fillets. This is best done in a blender. Beat in wine, which serves not only to smooth the sauce but to whiten it. Slice veal and lay slices, overlapping, on a serving platter. Cover with tuna sauce. Sprinkle with the remaining capers and garnish with half slices of lemon, boiled carrot slices and thin slices of gherkin. This sauce is also excellent on boiled beef.

Filet Mignon Piquant

Bistecche al piccantino

½ cup black olives	4 filet mignon steaks weighing about 6 oz each
3 anchovy fillets, chopped	
¾ cup chopped tomato pulp (skin and seeds removed and pulp chopped of fresh tomato)	3 tbsp olive oil
	2 tbsp capers
	½ cup dry white wine
	salt, pepper

Pit olives and chop coarsely. Mix olives, anchovy fillet and tomato pulp. Brown steaks quickly on both sides i oil and remove to a platter. Add tomato pulp mixtur and capers to pan juices. Heat until bubbly. Stir in win and a pinch of pepper and simmer until sauce is thic Season to taste with salt. Return steaks to pan and coo to desired degree, turning several times in sauce an making sure that they are not overcooked. Salt light and serve immediately with pan juices spooned ove them.

Veal with Mozzarella

Vitello alla mozzarella

6 slices boneless veal (or 12 small scallopini)	juice of ½ lemon
	6 slices prosciutto crudo
2 tbsp butter	6 slices mozzarella or scamorza
2 tbsp olive oil	
salt and pepper	

Pound veal slices, trim them so they are about the sam size and shape, then brown in butter and oil. Sprinkl with salt and pepper. Let meat cook to a golden browr then sprinkle with lemon juice. A few minutes befor serving, place a slice of prosciutto and one of mozzarell or scamorza on each veal slice. Heat until cheese mel and serve immediately.

Chicken Marengo

Roast Duck in Coarse Salt

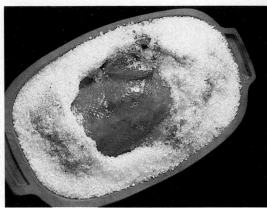

Chicken Marengo

Pollo alla Marengo

1 chicken (weighing approx. 2½ lbs) cut-up	1 small white truffle or black truffle, sliced
salt and pepper	1 small onion, sliced
¼ cup butter	1 bay leaf
¾ cup olive oil	1 rib celery, chopped
4 ripe tomatoes, peeled and sieved	pinch of thyme
	peppercorns
1 clove garlic, chopped	6 large crayfish or shrimp
6 sprigs parsley (chop 5 sprigs)	6 slices sandwich bread, crusts trimmed
2 cups dry white wine	6 eggs
½ lb wild "porcini" mushrooms	

Wash chicken and pat dry. Sprinkle with salt and pepper. Heat 1 tbsp of the butter and 6 tbsp of the oil in a large frying pan and brown pieces of chicken, turning to get all sides browned. Add tomatoes, garlic, half the chopped parsley. Boil half of the wine for 2 minutes, add to pan, cover and cook over moderate heat for 20 minutes. Meanwhile, cut off bottoms of mushroom stems (if you are using fresh wild mushrooms,) clean and slice. If using dried, soak in cold water then drain and chop. Put 2 tbsp of butter in a pan with 2 tbsp of the oil. Add mushrooms and truffle slices to pan. Sprinkle with salt and pepper and saute until wilted. Before removing from heat, sprinkle with remaining chopped parsley. Add mushrooms to chicken. Cover, simmer another 15 to 20 minutes or until chicken is tender. Heat remaining wine in a saucepan. Add onion, unchopped parsley sprig, bay leaf, celery, a pinch of thyme, several peppercorns and ½ tsp salt. When wine comes to a boil add shrimp and simmer for 5 minutes; drain and reserve shrimp. Shell and de-vein shrimp. Heat remaining oil in a frying pan and fry bread slices until brown on both sides. Heat remaining butter in a large frying pan and fry eggs until whites are firm and yolks still soft. Remove from heat and place fried eggs on slices of bread. Place chicken in centre of a large round serving dish. Spoon over pan juices. Place slices of bread with eggs around edges, alternating with shrimp.

Roast Duck in Coarse Salt

Anatra al sale

1 duckling weighing about 5 lbs.	coarse salt – sea salt, kosher salt, rock salt, 4 to 5 lb

Thaw duckling if frozen. Remove giblets and reserve fc making gravy. Truss to secure legs and wings to body Cover bottom of deep roasting pan with salt to a dept of ½ inch. Put duckling on salt and then cove completely with more salt. Press salt down on duckling Bake in a preheated oven 425°F for 1½ hours. Remov from oven, scrape salt off surface of duckling with spoon, then grasp trussing cord to lift duckling from sa bed with a quick decisive movement. Remove fina grains of salt with a pastry brush.

Duck Casserole

Anitra in salmi

1 duckling weighing about 5 lb	½ cup olive oil
1 medium onion	¼ cup wine vinegar
2 cloves	¼ cup dry white wine
1 bayleaf	parsley for garnish
2 sage leaves	salt and pepper

Joint the duckling. In a deep saucepan, place th chopped duck liver, heart and gizzard, the onion stuc with cloves, bayleaf and sage. Place the duck on top an pour over the olive oil, wine vinegar and white win Season with salt and pepper. Cover and simmer fc about 1 hour or until the duck is tender. Put the joints o a serving dish and keep warm. Remove the cloves an the bayleaf, and blend the remaining ingredients in th casserole with the cooking liquid. Return to the hea pour over the duck and garnish with chopped parsley.

Duck
Casserole

POULTRY

Chicken Livers with Peas

Chicken in Sweet-Sour Sauce

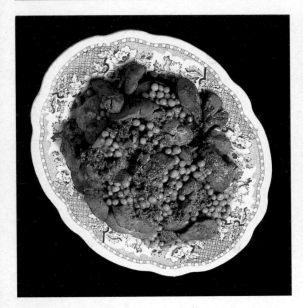

Chicken Livers with Peas

Fegatini di pollo con piselli

¾ lb chicken livers	½ cup chicken broth
2 cups shelled fresh green peas	4 slices of toast about ½-inch thick
5 tbsp butter	salt
3 tbsp chopped parsley	

Clean chicken livers and cut into halves or thirds. Cook peas in lightly salted boiling water until tender but still firm (al dente). Melt 3 tbsp of the butter in a saucepan, add peas, parsley. Then add chicken livers and broth. Stir frequently and cook for another 5 minutes. Toast bread in remaining butter, put them on a serving platter. Remove chicken livers and peas with a slotted spoon and spoon over toast. Keep warm. Boil pan juices over high heat reducing to half their original volume. Season to taste with salt. Pour over chicken livers.

Chicken in Sweet-Sour Sauce

Pollo in dolce-forte

1 chicken weighing about 4 lb	5 tbsp white wine vinegar
1 large onion	10 tbsp water
1 large carrot	1 bayleaf
15 juniper berries	4 tbsp olive oil
5 tbsp maraschino liqueur	salt and pepper

Joint the chicken. Marinate for several hours in th chopped onion, carrot, liqueur, vinegar, and wate juniper berries and bayleaf. Take the joints from th marinade, drain well. Saute in the olive oil until golde Place in a shallow casserole, add the unstraine marinade, cover and cook at 300°F for about 1 hour until the chicken is tender. Place on a warmed servir platter and keep warm. Remove the bayleaf and pre the cooking juices through a sieve. Reheat gently ar pour over the chicken to serve.

Capon with Garden Vegetables

Cappone 'sorpresa dell'ortolano'

1 capon weighing about 5 lb	1 cup white wine
2 slices pork fat	1 cup chicken broth
½ lb chicken livers, chopped	5 tbsp butter
½ lb prosciutto crudo, chopped	2 cups diced egg plant
salt and pepper	2 zucchini
¼ lb sliced bacon, chopped	2 green bell capsicum, cut into strips
2 carrots sliced	4 stalks celery, sliced
1 onion sliced	2 cups sliced mushrooms
bouquet garni of parsley, thyme and rosemary	2 cups chopped tomato pulp, skin and seeds removed

Cover legs of capon with pork fat. Stuff capon with liv and prosciutto. Sprinkle with salt and pepper and tru In a greased 3-quart shallow casserole put a layer bacon, carrots, onion and bouquet garni. Set capon this layer. Pour over wine and broth and roast in a p heated oven for 2 hours or until tender. Heat butter a saute eggplant, zucchini, capsicum and celery. After minutes add mushrooms and tomato pulp. Sprin with salt and pepper and continue cooking for minutes. Place capon on a platter. Press pan juic through a strainer and thicken if desired. Serve cap surrounded with vegetables. Spoon over pan juices.

Capon with Garden Vegetables

POULTRY

Chicken with Peppers

Chicken cooked in Milk

Chicken with Peppers

Pollo con peperoni

1 chicken (weighing about 2½ lbs)	salt, pepper
	½ cup dry white wine
4 to 5 fleshy green and red capsicum	4 cups fresh chopped tomato pulp, skins and seeds removed
1 large onion, sliced	
2 tbsp butter	1 cup chicken broth
3 tbsp olive oil	¼ cup chopped fresh basil

Cut chicken into serving pieces. Roast capsicum over heat until skin blisters. Rub skin off with a kitchen towel. Remove seeds and cut capsicum into 1-inch wide strips. Saute onion in butter and oil until wilted. Add chicken pieces and brown, turning often. Season with salt and pepper and, when chicken has browned, add wine. Simmer until wine has evaporated, add capsicum, tomatoes and another pinch of salt and pepper. Add broth. Cover and simmer over low heat stirring occasionally, for about 45 minutes or until chicken is tender. Remove from heat and sprinkle with chopped basil (or parsley if you prefer). Pan juices may be skimmed of fat and boiled until reduced to half their original volume. Pour pan juices over chicken.

Chicken cooked in Milk

Pollo al latte

1 chicken weighing about 4 lb	5 sprigs marjoram
2 tbsp olive oil	1 sprig basil
1 onion, chopped	1 bayleaf
1 carrot, chopped	salt and pepper
3¾ cups milk	slivered almonds to garnish
5 sprigs parsley	

In a large saucepan, brown the chicken in the hot oi Remove and set aside. Saute the onion and carrot for few minutes until beginning to brown. Return th chicken and pour over the milk. Add herbs an seasoning. Bring to the boil, cover and simmer ver gently for about 1 hour, until the chicken is tender. Plac chicken on a warmed serving platter. Keep warm Discard the bayleaf, and blend as much of the cookin juices with the carrot and onion and herbs as needed fo a sauce to serve with the chicken (it should be fairl thick). Cut the chicken into joints, pour over the sauc garnish with browned slivered almonds if wished.

Partridge "Gourmet Club"

Pernici "club del buongustaio"

¾ lb white beans (or haricot beans)	8 thin slices of pork fat
	¼ lb bacon
4 partridges	¼ cup covered prosciutto crudo
salt and pepper	
¼ cup butter	2 tbsp olive oil
5 tbsp goose liver, chopped	2 cups chopped tomato pulp, skin and seeds removed
5 tbsp truffles, chopped	

Boil beans in unsalted water until tender, about 2 hours. Split partridges in half. Flatten halves slightly by pounding gently. Remove and discard smallest bones, then season with salt and pepper. Heat butter in a larg frying pan. Brown halves on both sides. Drain and allov to cool. Stuff halves lightly with chopped goose liver an truffle. Wrap in pork fat. Put partridges back into pa juices. Set over heat and continue sauteing, turnin from time to time. Cook bacon in boiling water for hour. Remove and dice. Saute prosciutto in oil for minute. Add tomato pulp, season with salt and peppe and simmer for 10 minutes. Add drained beans, baco and simmer another 10 minutes. Put partridges on warmed platter, pour pan juices over and serve wit beans.

Partridge
"Gourmet Club"

POULTRY

Peas and Rice

Baked Asparagus Italian Style

Peas and Rice

Risi e bisi

⅓ cup bacon or prosciutto, as fat as possible	salt
½ onion, chopped	1½ quarts chicken broth
¼ cup butter	1 cup rice
1 tbsp olive oil	¼ cup grated Parmesan cheese
1 lb fresh peas	6 sprigs parsley, chopped

Risi e bisi is a famous dish from the Veneto region of Italy, and its title indicates that the proportion of peas and rice should be approximately equal. Saute chopped bacon and onion in half of the butter and oil. When onion is transparent, add peas; salt lightly, stir and add broth. Cover and cook over a moderate heat until the peas are half cooked. Add rice and stir with a wooden spoon, taking care not to crush the peas, and complete cooking. The rice will take about 17 minutes to cook. Before removing from the heat, stir in the remaining butter, Parmesan and parsley. Stir again, let stand for a few minutes and serve.

Baked Asparagus Italian Style

Asparagi in forno all'italiana

24 asparagus	¾ cup grated Parmesan
4 thick slices prosciutto crudo, fat and lean, or ham	4 slices toast (made by frying bread in butter)
6 tbsp butter	salt

Clean asparagus and trim tough ends. Remove scales. Tie asparagus in a bundle. Cook asparagus standing upright with tips above boiling water. Use your coffee pot for this. Drain while still al dente, untie the bundle and let asparagus cool completely. Wrap 6 asparagus tips in each slice of ham and arrange the rolls in a lightly buttered shallow baking dish. Pour about 2 tbsp of melted butter over them, sprinkle with grated Parmesan, then pour 1 tbsp more melted butter over the Parmesan. Put the dish in a preheated oven 400°F and bake until surface is well browned, about 15 minutes. Meanwhile brown bread slices in remaining butter and transfer them to a serving dish. Put ham asparagus rolls on each slice of toast and serve.

Stuffed Tomatoes Home-Style

Pomodori casalinghi ripieni

8 medium tomatoes	A few basil leaves, chopped
salt and pepper	6 sprigs parsley, chopped
1 small onion, chopped	2 anchovy fillets
9 tbsp butter	¼ cup pine nuts, ground in a mortar
3 cups soft breadcrumbs	
½ cup grated Parmesan	

Cut a thin slice off the tops of the tomatoes. Scoop out the seeds, then squeeze tomato cups lightly over a bowl to catch juice. Sprinkle tomato cups lightly with salt and invert them on a rack set over a pan. Reserve juice. Saute onion in ¼ cup of the butter until golden. Combine onion and drippings, breadcrumbs, grated Parmesan, basil, parsley, anchovy fillets and pine nuts. Sprinkle with salt and pepper and stir in reserved tomato juice. Mix well. Arrange tomato cups side by side in a buttered baking dish, stuff with filling. Dot with remaining butter and bake in a pre-heated oven 350°F for 20 minutes or until tomatoes are tender but still hold their shape.

Stuffed Tomatoes
Home-Style

VEGETABLES

Sauteed Sliced Artichoke Bottoms with Parsley and Garlic

Buttered Fennel with Ham

Sauteed Sliced Artichoke Bottoms with Parsley and Garlic

Fondi di carciofo trifolati

8 large artichokes	salt, pepper
2 cloves garlic, chopped	6 sprigs parsley, chopped
7 tbsp olive oil	

Remove all the artichoke leaves and trim off choke, leaving only the fleshy bottom of the artichoke. Slice artichoke bottoms into strips. Saute garlic in oil briefly, then add artichoke bottoms and season with salt and pepper. Cook for several minutes over high heat, then lower heat and continue cooking until artichokes are tender, about 30 minutes. Sprinkle finely chopped parsley over dish just before serving.

Buttered Fennel with Ham

Finocchi al burro con prosciutto

4 fennel roots ("finocchi")	2 cups chicken broth
1/4 cup butter	salt
1 small onion, chopped fine	1/2 cup grated Parmesan
3/4 cup chopped baked or boiled ham	

Discard harsh outer layers of fennel. Remove stems o fennel and cut them into wedges. Heat butter and saut onion. Add ham with fennel and cook over low heat fo about 10 minutes. Add broth and cook at a boil unt broth is evaporated. Season to taste with salt. Sprinkl grated Parmesan over fennel, remove from heat an serve.

Stuffed Zucchini

Zucchini Ripieni

3 1/2 lbs zucchini (12 small or 6 large)	2/3 cup grated Parmesan cheese
1/2 cup diced cooked ham	2 eggs
2 tbsp chopped parsley	nutmeg
1/4 cup chopped fresh basil leaves	salt, pepper
2 tbsp dry bread crumbs, approx.	5 tbsp butter
	1 tbsp flour
	1 cup milk

Cut ends off zucchini and trim them to same length. Wash and drain. Boil zucchini in lightly salted water for 10 minutes or until half cooked. Drain. Slice in half lengthwise and remove pulp, reserving it in a bowl. Reserve shells (1/2-inch thick.) Mix ham, parsley and basil with chopped zucchini pulp. Add bread crumbs, all of the grated Parmesan except for 2 tbsp, eggs, freshly grated nutmeg and salt and pepper to taste. Mix thes ingredients thoroughly and set aside. Melt 1/4 cup of th butter and stir in flour. Gradually stir in milk. Stir ove low heat until sauce bubbles and thickens. Stir sauc into zucchini mixture. Add more bread crumbs if mixtur is not thick enough to spoon. Using a spoon fill zucchir shells with mixture. Arrange them side by side in a but tered (use remaining butter) shallow baking dish Sprinkle with remaining grated Parmesan and bake in pre-heated oven 350°F for 1/2 hour. Serve hot in bakin dish.

Stuffed
Zucchini

VEGETABLES

Deep Dish Pear Pie Piedmont style

Caramelized Oranges

Deep Dish Pear Pie Piedmont Style

Timballo con le pere alla piemontese

For pie-crust:
1¾ cups sifted all-purpose
    flour
salt
½ cup yellow cornmeal
⅔ cup fine sugar
½ cup butter
3 egg yolks

For filling:
6 large firm cooking pears
½ cup sugar
½ cup red wine
1 whole clove
pinch cinnamon

In a saucepan mix pears, sugar, wine, clove, and cinnamon. Simmer for 15 minutes or until pears are almost tender. Cool. In a bowl mix flour, pinch salt, cornmeal and sugar. Cut in butter (reserving 1 tbsp) until particles are very fine. Stir in egg yolks and if necessary, a little water to make a stiff dough. Knead a few times on a floured surface until a smooth ball. Let it stand covered for 30 minutes. Roll out ⅔ of the dough into a sheet large enough to line the bottom and sides of an ungreased 8″ pie pan.

    Drain pears. Pour pears into lined pie pan. Roll out remaining crust and place over filling. Crimp edges to seal. Prick top. Bake in a preheated oven until well browned and crisp, about 35-40 minutes. Serve hot.

Caramelized Oranges

Arance caramellizzate

6 oranges
1 lemon
½ lb sugar

1¼ cups water
1 tbsp kirsch

Peel the oranges, carefully, cut away all the pith. Reserv[e] some peel. Boil the sugar and water to make a ligh[t] syrup. Dip the fruit in the syrup. Put the fruit in a bow[l]. Cut the reserved peel into thin matchsticks and cook i[n] vigorously boiling water for a few minutes. Strain. Pu[t] the syrup in a small pan and simmer the peel in this un[til] it becomes transparent and caramelized. Allow to coo[l] and stir in the kirsch. Slice all the fruit, put in a servin[g] dish. Arrange the peel neatly on top, and pour the syru[p] over it.

Lemon Water Ice

Gelato di limone

5 lemons
4½ cups water

1 lb sugar

Heat the water and sugar over a moderate heat for [5] minutes. Bring to a boil for 5 minutes. Allow to cool.

    Add grated lemon zest to the syrup, together with th[e] lemon juice. Stir well and leave for 30 minutes. Strain[,] pour into a container and freeze until the ice starts to se[t]. Beat well and return to the freezer. Remove from th[e] freezer 10-15 minutes before serving.

Lemon
Water Ice

SWEETS

Mont Blanc with Marrons Glacés

Baked Stuffed Peaches

Mont Blanc with Marrons Glacés

Montebianco con marrons glacés

2½ lb chestnuts	sugar
milk	1 cup heavy cream, whipped
1 tsp vanilla	Marrons glacés

Slit chestnuts and cover with water. Boil for about 30 minutes, drain and peel, removing shell and brown inner skin. Cover chestnuts with milk in a saucepan. Add vanilla and bring to boiling point. Cover and cook over low heat for about 45 minutes or until chestnuts are tender and mealy. Stir occasionally to prevent sticking. Drain, mash chestnuts in a food mill. Measure puree and add half the amount of sugar. In a saucepan set puree over moderate heat and, stirring constantly, cook until mixture becomes thick and pulls away from sides of saucepan, about 30 minutes. Remove from heat and let it cool completely. Put puree in a potato ricer and press chestnuts through, letting them fall in a mound onto serving plate. Cover this with whipped cream and garnish with marrons glacés. Chill until ready to serve.

Baked Stuffed Peaches

Pesche in tegame

4 large firm but ripe peaches	5 bitter almond macaroons,
½ cup sugar	crumbled
grated rind of 1 lemon	1 egg yolk
2 tbsp bitter cocoa	peach liqueur
¼ cup blanched almonds,	2 tbsp butter
chopped	

Peel peaches, split in half and remove pits. Scoop out some of the peach leaving a shell 1″ thick. Put pulp removed in a bowl. Add half the sugar, lemon rind, cocoa, almonds, macaroons and egg yolk. Mix with enough liqueur to form a thick paste. Stuff peach halves with this filling, arrange them in a baking dish, dot with butter, sprinkle with remaining sugar and bake in a preheated oven for 25-30 minutes, or until peaches are tender and still hold their shape.

Sicilian Cheese Cake

Cassata alla siciliana

1½ lbs ricotta cheese, sieved	½ cup chopped candied
1 cup sugar	fruits
triple sec liqueur	1 "4 egg" Genoise cake
½ cup bitter chocolate,	Cognac
coarsely grated	

Mix ricotta and sugar until creamy. Remove half a cup and set aside for top of cake. Add 1 tbsp liqueur to remaining cheese along with chocolate and candied fruits. Chill mixture for 30 minutes. Using a serrated knife, cut sponge cake into ½″ thick slices. Take a loaf pan and line with wax paper. Mix equal parts cognac and liqueur. Dip sponge cake slices lightly in mixture and line bottom and sides of loaf pan. (Be careful not to over soak cake otherwise it will fall apart.) Pour in ricotta mixture, pressing it down and levelling it with a spatula. On top put a layer of remaining sponge cake moistened with cognac-liqueur mixture. Chill for a few hours.

When ready to serve, turn cassata out upside down on a platter; if it doesn't come out easily, immerse pan briefly in boiling water. Remove wax paper, cover cassata with reserved ricotta and serve.

Sicilian
Cheese Cake

SWEETS

INDEX

The publishers would like to express their thanks to MRS. SHERRIE SORENSEN, who kindly prepared the dishes and provided facilities for photography. Photography by Neil Sutherland.

First published in Great Britain 1983 by Colour Library Books Ltd.
© 1983 Illustrations and text: Colour Library Books Ltd. Guildford, Surrey, England.
Photoset by The Printed Word Ltd. London, England.
Colour separations by Reprocolor Llovet, S.A.
Printed by Cayfosa, bound by Eurobinder in Barcelona, Spain
All rights reserved.
ISBN 0-86283-099-0
COLOUR LIBRARY BOOKS